Carl Reinecke

SONATA (*UNDINE*) OP. 167

for Flute and Piano

Edited by

JAMES GALWAY

Piano Part Edited by Phillip Moll

Ed. 3369

GREAT PERFORMER'S EDITION

G. SCHIRMER, *Inc.*

DISTRIBUTED BY
HAL•LEONARD® CORPORATION
7777 W. BLUEMOUND RD. P.O. BOX 13819 MILWAUKEE, WI 53213

The Story of Undine

The Undine legend concerns the ill-fated union of a beautiful water-nymph with Huldebrand, a young knight. Only by winning the true love of a mortal man can Undine hope to acquire an immortal soul. Her father, a powerful underwater prince, desires this for her and substitutes her while she is still a small child for the only daughter of a pious fisherman, assigning Undine's uncle Kühleborn to oversee her development from a discreet distance. The fisherman's true daughter Berthalda is found on a distant shore by a nobleman and raised by him in opulent surroundings, unaware of her humble background.

Some years later, when Undine and Berthalda are grown up, the latter is courted by Huldebrand. She sends him on a quest in an enchanted forest. Kühleborn arranges for a storm to maroon Huldebrand on the peninsula where the fisherman lives. Huldebrand falls in love with Undine and marries her. When the storm has abated he brings her back to his castle. She pledges her love but warns him never to reproach her over a body of water, for then she would be compelled by the water-spirits to leave him.

Berthalda is vexed by this turn of events but befriends Undine and comes to live at the castle. Huldebrand begins to flirt with her and to disparage Undine's acquatic origins. This threat to his niece's happiness is not to Kühleborn's liking. Undine, in order to thwart provocative tactics on the part of her uncle which might displease Huldebrand, has the well sealed off.

Nevertheless, when the three are sailing on the Danube Kühleborn disrupts their enjoyment with waves and storms, finally reaching up from the water to snatch from Berthalda a golden necklace Huldebrand had given her. Undine dives down and returns with a beautiful ring of coral to replace it. Enraged, Huldebrand flings the coral back into the river and tells Undine to go back where she belongs and "leave us humans in peace." With heavy heart she disappears beneath the waves, not before lovingly exhorting her husband to remain true to her; otherwise, he must die.

Ignoring Undine's warning, Huldebrand and Berthalda prepare to marry. On their wedding night, while Huldebrand awaits Berthalda in his room, Undine emerges from the reopened well and appears to him, now having no alternative but to fulfill the law of her underwater folk. Lifting her veil, she tearfully enfolds Huldebrand in a loving embrace until his beath leaves him and he sinks onto the bed.

After Huldebrand's funeral a bubbling spring forms around the mound where he lies buried. Local inhabitants say this is the arms of Undine forever encircling her beloved.

* * *

This tale achieved great popularity in the 19th century in a version by Friedrich de la Motte Fouqué, which would have been familiar to Reinecke. The flute sonata is not program music, it does not describe the events described above; its relation to the story is allusive, rather than narrative. Apart from the plot, Reinecke must have seen polarities in the story which were useful to him in generating musical contrasts within the sonata form. Among these might be the magical versus the natural; the underwater kingdom versus the world of men; the free spirit of the water-nymph versus the pain and longing which accompany her experience of humanity; and her unwavering loyalty versus the reality of a world of imperfection and confiicting passions. The listener will not derive the story from hearing the sonata, but familiarity with the story can help performers find the proper spirit and atmosphere in this highly colorful music.

Phillip Moll
April, 1983

SONATA
(UNDINE)

CARL REINECKE, Op. 167
Edited by James Galway
Piano Part Edited by Phillip Moll

2
mf
p
mf
p
mf
Ped.
Ped.
mf espressivo
pp
Ped.
Ped.
dolce
Ped.
Ped.

espressivo
dolce
dim.
3
p dolce
mf
sempre p
sf
pp
Ped.

4
mf
Ped.
p
f
decresc.
espressivo

5
p
Ped.
cresc.
più f
f
decrescendo
mf espressivo
espressivo

mf
Ped.
crescendo
cresc. poco a poco
poco
a
poco
f
6
f
p
marcato

mf
cresc.
Ped.
7
f
mf
cresc.

f
f
decresc
8
p dolce
pp
espressivo
mf
Ped.
Ped.
Ped.

*The hand-crossings are suggested by Reinecke. The editor prefers to play both of these notes with the right hand.

Intermezzo

Allegretto vivace ♩=120

p
Ped.
1
sf
f
mf
p calando

Ped.
p
pp
cresc.

f
mf
Ped.
p
senza vibrato
p e misterioso
dolce
3
Più lento, quasi Andante
pp

FLUTE

SONATA
(UNDINE)

CARL REINECKE, Op. 167
Edited by James Galway
Piano Part Edited by Phillip Moll

decresc.
5
più f
3
cresc. poco a poco
2
6
2

3
7
mf
f
mf
6
f
8
p
dolce
11
9
dolce
pp
p
pp
Intermezzo
Allegretto vivace ♩ = 120
f
mf
decresc.
p
f
pp
p
mf
p
p
sf

*The editor prefers to play this section with vibrato.

5 Andante tranquillo ♩= 84
p dolce
6
cre - scen - do
calando
a tempo
accel
7 Molto vivace ♩= 88
tr
fp
pp
sf

8 Tempo primo
p dolce
p
3
pp
Finale
Allegro molto 𝅗𝅥 = 152
f
dolce
4
f con fuoco
ff
p
mf
1
cresc.
con fuoco
dolce
molto
un poco calando
tranquillo
2
mf

cresc. molto
ff
mf
f
2
3
ff con fuoco
4
ff
3
p
f con fuoco cresc.
4
con fuoco
dolce
f
4
f
5
5
p
4
f
dolce
dolce
poco calando
4

6
f
7
Più animato
3
2
ff con tutta la forza
sf
p
rall.
8
Più lento
10
pp e misterioso
sempre pp
pp
ppp

ppp
mf
dim.
④ Intermezzo
Allegretto vivace ♩=120
f
sf
mf
ten.

espr.

5
Andante tranquillo ♩ = 84
p dolce
p dolce
Ped.
f
p
mf
p
cresc. molto
6
f
p
cre -
scen - - - - - do
cresc.
f
f
calando
calando
a tempo
a tempo
pp

mf
f
pp
p
accelerando molto
7
Molto vivace 𝅗𝅥 = 88
pp e mormorando
sfp
fp
p

pp
sfp
Ped.
fp
8
Tempo I
sf
dolce
p dolce
p
mf cresc.
f
pp
calando

Finale

Allegro molto agitato ed appassionato, quasi Presto ♩ = 152

p
mf
cresc.
Ped.
f
dolce
cresc.
ff
f con fuoco
mf

dolce
cresc. molto
dolce
f
f
f con fuoco
mf
dolce
dolce
un poco calando
cresc.
un poco ca-

Un poco più tranquillo
2
calando
calando
dolce
mf
cresc. molto
cresc.
ff
mf
f
con fuoco
Ped.

ff con
Ped.
3
fuoco
con passione
ff
Ped.
ff
Ped.
decresc.
Ped.
p

p
espressivo
f
con fuoco
cresc.
4
con fuoco
mf
dolce
dolce

ff con fuoco
Ped.
5

f
dolce
dolce
Ped.
dolce

poco calando
dolce
f ma dolce
Ped.
6
f
ff con fuoco

7
Più mosso
p
cresc.
f
ff con tutta la forza
8
Più lento
rall.
pp
una corda

pp e misterioso
sempre pp
pp
ppp
pp
ppp